The Tiswas Book of Ghastly Ghosts

The sound of a shoe on wood, or a shoe on stone—that is easy to explain, but the sound that Martin and Blunden heard wasn't like either of these! The steps were soft, but there was also a scratching sound—just like an animal's claws or a bird's talons. Martin and Blunden looked at each other in terror. Whatever was walking up the stairs and towards their room, certainly wasn't human!

Whether you believe in ghosts or not, all the people featured in this book certain do—because they *saw* one. . . .

Treat yourself to

THE TISWAS BOOK OF SILLY SUPERSTITIONS

also published by CAROUSEL BOOKS

THE TISWAS BOOK OF GHASTLY GHOSTS

A CAROUSEL BOOK   0   552   54186   9

First published in Great Britain by Carousel Books

PRINTING HISTORY
Carousel edition published 1981

Copyright © 1981 ATV Network Ltd.
Compilation copyright © 1981 Helen Piddock
Illustrations copyright © 1981 Transworld Publishers Ltd.

Carousel Books are published by
Transworld Publishers Ltd.,
Century House, 61–63 Uxbridge Road,
Ealing, London W5 5SA.

Made and printed in Great Britain by Cox & Wyman Ltd.,
Reading.

THE TISWAS BOOK
OF GHASTLY GHOSTS

Compiled by

Helen Piddock

Illustrated by

Daniel Woods

CAROUSEL BOOKS

Before You Begin...

Clanking chains, eerie sounds, vanishing people, screams in the dark, and things that go bump in the night! All the ingredients to make a jolly good frightening story! If you like your hair to stand on end, your flesh to creep and your skin to come out in goose bumps, then this is the book for you! Whether you believe in ghosts or not, all the people featured in this book certainly do because they *saw* one!

All of us on the Tiswas team enjoy a good ghost story so we've collected together some of our favourites which we hope you will like as much as we do? If "like" is the right word! ! ! We've done a lot of research to find additional facts about some famous ghost stories, but we've also come across a few that nobody has written about before. The most frightening thing we discovered about the "new" ghosts is that they were seen very recently, in fact one, "Emma", is still being seen today and will probably continue to appear in the future. Scary isn't it?

Before you start reading this book, may we please give you a set of rules which you ought to follow:

1) **Always read this book in a room with all the lights on.**

2) If reading this in bed, check that nothing is under the bed and the windows are firmly shut.

3) Before you start reading, check that nobody is likely to walk into the room very suddenly.

4) Don't attempt to read this book if you are nervous or don't like being frightened.

Happy reading! !

CONTENTS

Ghosts Seen in Modern Times

Sea Ghosts

Famous Ghosts

Odd Ghosts

THE ROCKING
WARDROBE

*If you think that all ghost stories happened in
the dim distant past, well you'd better think again!
Here's one that took place in 1958 in a small
village in central Wales.*

Beth Clements had been orphaned during the
Second World War when both her parents were
killed. She'd been left the family farm, but when
she married Hywell Parry, a city boy, born and
brought up in Cardiff, they decided to convert the
house into a hotel. It took a long time, and was also
a great deal more expensive than they'd imagined,
but by 1955 they had converted most of the rooms
and could take in ten paying guests. The rest of the
large, rambling farmhouse, they decided to leave
until they'd established a regular stream of book-
ings.

9

April, 1955, was the first time that retired school-master, William Benyon, went to stay. He was very fond of walking so found this comfortable family hotel, in the heart of the Welsh countryside, an ideal place to use as a base. He stayed there twice during 1955, two weeks each visit, then again in April and May 1956 and 1957. In 1958, it was a very wet April so for part of his stay he was the only guest in the hotel. By this time he was quite friendly with the Parry's and, when they weren't busy, they tended to treat him as one of the family rather than a paying guest.

On the first Wednesday of his visit the weather cleared enough for him to be out all day walking. When he returned he tucked into a hearty meal then retired for an early night.

When he stayed at the hotel, he always had the same room. All the rooms were large and airy, but Number 6 also had a large picture window with an uninterrupted view of a range of hills. The farm-house was, in part, two hundred years old. Other bits had been added on over the years but Number 6 was in the very old part. Consequently the ceiling was rather low and the floor sloped, but William Benyon preferred it to the more modern rooms because he said it had "charm". This "charm" meant that the floorboards creaked and guests had to duck their heads under some of the beams. It also meant the wind was able to creep through some of the cracks in the window frames, but with plenty of blankets on the bed, Mr. Benyon never once com-plained of the cold.

On this particular night, Mr. Benyon read in bed for a short time then, tired out by his long walk and the good food he'd eaten, he floated off into a very heavy sleep. There was no wind that night so he was very surprised, some hours later, to find himself woken by an icy breeze. He sat up and looked towards the window to see if it had somehow been blown open. He always kept his curtains open, so he could see that the window was still firmly closed. The curtains were also flat against the wall, so where could the cold wind be coming from? He looked across the room to the door, but that, too, was firmly closed. The chill was beginning to bite into his bones so he lay down and pulled the blankets tight around him. He tried to get back to sleep but the cold was becoming so intense that he started shivering, violently.

After ten minutes of shivering, Mr. Benyon decided he couldn't bear the cold any longer. He got up to turn on the gas fire, and also put on some extra clothes. But as he was moving round the room, he had the distinct feeling that someone else was in the room. He looked around but nobody was there. Dismissing the feeling as nothing but the effect of the cold, he got back into bed.

He slept badly for the rest of the night, mainly because the coldness disappeared and he'd got so many clothes on that he was boiling hot.

Next morning at breakfast, he told the Parrys about the strange changes in temperature. But they said they'd had a good night's sleep and that the weather had been quite mild. Mr. Benyon was puzzled.

"Has anything like that ever happened before?" he asked.

Hywell Parry shook his head. "Not that I know of. No guest has ever mentioned anything like it to me. But I'll check the heating and the windows in your room, if you like?"

Mr. Benyon thanked him, then left the hotel for

11

his daily walk.

That night the same thing happened.

Mr. Benyon woke up, shivering violently from the cold. Once again he got out of bed and put the fire on, and also some extra clothes and blankets. But this time he was even more sure that someone was in the room with him. Nobody was there!

Mr. Benyon was a very down-to-earth sort of man, not usually given to letting his imagination run free. He also firmly believed that there were no such things as ghosts, but in this instance he was convinced that there was something "odd" going on!

Next day he told the Parrys about his feelings, and asked if there were any stories about a possible ghost in the farmhouse?

Hywell Parry laughed loudly. "You don't believe any of that old rubbish?"

"No, I don't," replied Mr. Benyon, "but how else do you explain my feeling that someone else was in the room when no-one was there?"

Hywell shrugged. "Not meaning to be rude Mr. Benyon, but you haven't been reading any funny books have you?"

Mr. Benyon shook his head.

Beth Parry chided her husband, "You don't know everything Hywell Parry, how do you know there are no such things as ghosts?"

Her husband laughed. "The day you show me a real live ghost is the day that I'll believe in them. Until then, the whole thing's a load of stuff and nonsense."

Mr. Benyon didn't want to start an argument between husband and wife and, saying he must have imagined it all, he left the hotel for the morning.

That night Mr. Benyon couldn't get to sleep. He

lay in his bed tossing and turning, so this time when the temperature changed, he was already awake. Once again he turned on the fire and added extra clothes, and once again he could sense someone in the room with him. He wasn't scared, just interested. He turned on the light to double-check that the room was empty but this time he thought he saw something!

On the other side of the room was a very large wardrobe and, just to one side of it, Mr. Benyon was positive that he could see something! It wasn't a figure, it wasn't a shadow, it was just *something*! But if Mr. Benyon doubted his eyes and perhaps his mind, he was in no doubt when the wardrobe began to shake. As clear as anything, he could see the huge wardrobe slowly starting to rock! From side to side it moved, the old wood creaking and groaning!

Then, as suddenly as it had started, the wardrobe stopped moving. At exactly the same time the room became warm and, whatever it was that Mr. Benyon thought he'd seen, had vanished!

This time Mr. Benyon didn't mention the event to the Parrys. He decided to keep it to himself until something else happened, which didn't seem unlikely, to avoid Mr. Parry's scorn and laughter.

He didn't have long to wait!

The next night was Saturday and the hotel had quite a number of weekend visitors. But the hotel being full made no difference to Mr. Benyon's "vistor". Exactly the same thing happened as on the previous night. It happened again on the Sunday, the Monday and the Tuesday. Each time the figure grew slightly more distinct and the wardrobe rocked harder!

13

By Wednesday night, one week since the strange happenings had begun, Mr. Benyon could definitely make out the figure of a man! There were no sharp edges to the form, just a shadowy, indefinite shape! *And the man was pushing the wardrobe.* The first time Mr. Benyon had seen the wardrobe rocking, there had been no proof of the event in the morning. But by Wednesday he could see that the wardrobe had actually moved a few centimetres! It was an incredibly heavy wardrobe, and he could see why so much effort was needed to shift it!

On Thursday morning he decided to show the Parrys the wardrobe's new position but they had gone out for the day before he had a chance to take them upstairs. That evening when they returned, he decided to leave it one more night, because the "proof" might be even more obvious by the next morning! But if "proof" was what he was after, that night he had more "proof" of his ghostly visitor than he could ever have dreamed!

As usual he woke up in the middle of the night because of the change in temperature. But this time, far from being cold, it was boiling hot! He sat up and gasped in the stifling heat. As he turned on the light, his whole body froze with terror at the sight of a man standing at the foot of his bed. He was tall and thin, and was anxiously rubbing his hands together. Was he another guest who'd wandered into his room by mistake? Mr. Benyon was sure he'd never seen him before. He was about to ask the stranger what he wanted when the man spoke.

"I need your help!"

Mr. Benyon stared at him in amazement.

"I need your help," he said again. "We must move that wardrobe."

The man turned to the wardrobe and started to

14

push it.

Not really thinking what he was doing, Mr. Benyon found himself out of bed and standing by the stranger as they both strained against the wardrobe.

With two of them pushing it, the wardrobe soon began to move. After about five minutes they'd shoved it sufficiently away from the wall to reveal a door that had been hidden behind it.

By this time the heat was intense! Mr. Benyon was startled at the sight of the door, but even more startled by the fact that he hadn't even questioned what he was doing.

The man then moved to the bedroom door opening onto the corridor and flung it back. As he did so the heat seemed to sweep into the room like an enormous wave.

Mr. Benyon raced to the open door and was horrified by what he saw. At the far end of the corridor, just past the top of the stairs, a fire door had been installed as a division between the corridor that housed bedrooms 3 to 10, Mr. Benyon's corridor, and bedrooms 1 and 2 along with the Parry's private quarters. The fire door was partly glass and Mr. Benyon could see that the corridor on the other side was swamped with flames. Smoke was seeping under the door and the heat was nearly unbearable. He could tell that it was just a matter of minutes before the door would give way under the force of the flames.

"The Parrys!" he exclaimed. "Where are they?"

"They are trapped in their rooms," was the reply. "That is the only staircase and they cannot get to it."

"What are we going to do?" exclaimed Mr. Benyon.

"Follow me," said the man, and walking back to

15

the wardrobe he squeezed behind it to the hidden door. He unlatched it and went through. Mr. Benyon followed and found himself in a large empty room with another door on the far side. He followed the man across the floor and through the other door. He now found himself in a corridor running parallel to the main corridor that lead to his bedroom. It was obviously a part of the large house that the Parrys hadn't got round to renovating. There were a number of doors leading off the corridor on the left and one more door at the far end.

The man strode down the corridor to the first door on the left. He opened it. Mr. Benyon could see a rickety old staircase leading down the outside of the building.

"This is the only way the Parrys can escape," said the stranger, then pointed to the door at the far end of the corridor. "That door leads into their private quarters. It's locked. It's too strong a door for them to break down, which is why you must open it."

"But how?" shouted Mr. Benyon. "*I'm* not strong enough to break it down."

The man put his hand into a pocket and took out a large key. Without hesitating Mr. Benyon grabbed it and ran down the corridor. With trembling fingers he managed to insert the key in the lock, and turned it. It worked! He pulled open the door and found himself in a tiny corridor. On his right was another fire door which led to bedroom's 1 and 2. It was only just holding back the roaring flames. Opposite him was a door leading to the Parry's bedroom. He threw it open and ran in.

Astonished, he saw Mr. and Mrs. Parry asleep in bed. He ran over and grabbed at Hywell.

16

"Get up, get up!" he screamed. "The house is on fire!"

The Parrys sat up and looked in astonishment at Mr. Benyon.

"The house is on fire!" he repeated. "You must follow me."

By this time the Parrys could feel the heat, and without question they leapt out of bed and followed Mr. Benyon. He took them back through the large door and down the disused corridor. He lead them through the outside door and down the rickety staircase, then across the back lawn until they were safely away from the burning house.

There was no sign of the stranger!

Nobody knew who'd phoned the fire-brigade, but only moments after Mr. Benyon and the Parrys had escaped, the fire engines arrived and the hoses were in action. They worked amazingly quickly and effectively with the result that most of the farmhouse was saved. Nearly all the bedrooms were affected, but bedrooms 1 and 2 and the Parry's quarters were completely gutted. There was no doubt about it, Mr. Benyon had saved their lives!

After it was all over, Mr. Benyon tried to explain what happened. The Parrys listened to him in total amazement because they said the back corridor hadn't been used for years since it was unsafe! When they'd got enough money they were planning to do something with it, but that was to be many years ahead. The big door had been locked about four years earlier and they'd lost the key, so how did the man have it? Who was the man? All the weekend guests had left on the Sunday. How did the man know about the back corridor? How did he know about the wardrobe?

17

Mr. Benyon tried to describe the "man". He was tall, about a head taller than himself, and quite a slim build. He had dark hair going grey at the sides and thin on top. Mr. Benyon tried hard to remember what he looked like, but found it very difficult. The image was, at the most, hazy. "His face was, well, thin, but he did have a small moustache."

As soon as he said this, Beth Parry cried out. "A moustache? You're sure he had a moustache?"

"Why, yes," said Mr. Benyon, "it was a grey one."

Beth looked at her husband, a strange expression on her face. "Can you remember what his clothes were like?" she asked quietly.

"He was wearing a sort of tweed jacket, mainly brown I think." Mr. Benyon was getting puzzled by the Parry's reaction to his description. "Do you think you know who he is?"

Hywell Parry was looking at his wife with an equally strange expression. "Can you remember anything else about him?" he asked in a low, hoarse voice.

Mr. Benyon thought hard. "There was something odd about his neck, or rather, he had something round it. I think it was a sort of scarf or muffler."

"Could you guess his age?" whispered Beth.

"About forty, maybe forty-five."

By this time both the Parry's had gone white. Beth was shaking and her eyes staring in horror.

"What's the matter?" exclaimed Mr. Benyon, more than alarmed by the effects of his words.

Hywell Parry slowly started to speak. "Yes, I think we know who your stranger is, or rather, was! Four years ago we started work on that back corridor. We employed a builder called Yian Phillips. Because the floorboards were unsafe we kept that end door locked, and Yian always kept the key. One day there was an accident." At this point in the story Beth Parry started to cry. Putting his arm round her to comfort her, Hywell continued falteringly with his tale. "Yian fell through a rotten floor-board. He landed in the old stables underneath. He was killed. We haven't been along that corridor since."

Mr. Benyon looked puzzled. "But what has that got to do with last night's stranger?"

"Your description exactly fits Yian Phillips. He had the key, and only he knew about that corridor, the doors and the outside staircase."

"You mean the man who showed me the way last night, has been dead for four years?"

Hywell Parry nodded his head.

It was at this point Mr. Benyon decided to tell the Parry's about his strange experiences during the nights of the past week. At the end of his story all three of them were convinced that the nightly visitor had been the ghost of Yian Phillips who somehow knew the fire was going to happen, and had "come back" to do his best to help.

They sat in silence for many minutes, thinking over what had happened to them.

Suddenly Hywell spoke. "But there's something that doesn't fit." He turned to Mr. Benyon. "Are you saying that the ghost pushed away the wardrobe to reveal a door that lead into another room?" Mr. Benyon nodded. "And that he took you across that room to a door on the other side which lead to the back corridor?" Again Mr. Benyon nodded. "But that's impossible! When Yian had repaired the floor of the back corridor, his next job was to replace the floor of that room."

"What do you mean, 'replace' it?" asked Mr. Benyon.

"There isn't a floor there. The entire floor collapsed about twenty years ago. There are no beams, no floor boards, no nothing! Just an empty space leading down to the old grain store beneath."

The three looked at each other in astonishment! Then slowly, without saying a word, they made their way upstairs to the main corridor. Everything was black from the fire, but it was safe to walk along. They came to the door of bedroom number 6 and went in. The wardrobe was just as it had been left the night before. Mr. Benyon pushed past it and opened the once hidden door.

He looked into the room that he had walked across the night before.

There were no floorboards, no beams, nothing! *Only an empty space that dropped five metres to the grain store below!*

Diagram of the house—second floor.

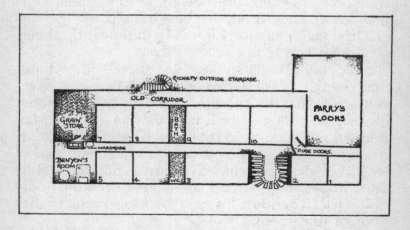

EMMA

*A few kilometres outside Worcester there is a
small village called Hanbury. There are so many
ghost stories about the parish that we could have
written an entire book on the one place. But, because we wanted variety, we decided to pick just
one story, and the one we've chosen happened very
recently in 1980.*

Hanbury Parish Church is situated high on a hill.
In the olden days, people used to go to church by
carriage but, because the hill was too steep for their
horses, a coach house was built at the bottom of the
hill so the horses could be looked after during the
service.

As the years went by the coach house was no
longer needed and gradually fell into disrepair. In

21

1980, a couple called Rudge decided to buy the coach house and do it up for their own use. While the work was being done they couldn't live in the house, so they bought a caravan and parked it in the garden.

One night Mrs. Rudge was sitting in the caravan when she was startled by a face at the window. She didn't recognise it and after a few moments it disappeared. She went outside the caravan but there was nobody there. Being a very sensible and calm woman, she just dismissed the event as being "a nosy neighbour"!

A few nights later the same thing happened. This time Mrs. Rudge could see the face more clearly. It was definitely a woman with long straggly hair. Mrs. Rudge waited for the woman to move, but she didn't. Although Mrs. Rudge was sure that the woman could see she was being looked at, the face stayed where it was for some time before it vanished as if into thin air. This time Mrs. Rudge wasn't quite so happy about the event and told her husband about it. He was inclined to scoff at the whole thing and say that his wife must have imagined it, but Mrs. Rudge was certain that it had really happened.

Three nights later the face reappeared. This time Mrs. Rudge quickly opened the caravan door, but whoever it was had disappeared again.

The same thing occurred the next night, and the next and the next. By now Mrs. Rudge was convinced that she was seeing some sort of ghost or apparition, but because the face didn't appear to mean her any harm, she didn't worry about it.

Then something else happened!

One night Mrs. Rudge was quietly doing some sewing when she had the distinct impression that someone was in the caravan with her. It was quite a large van with a number of small rooms, so she quickly opened all the doors to see if anyone was there. The van was empty. She continued her sewing but grew increasingly certain she wasn't alone.

When she told her husband about it, later, he asked if she'd been frightened by the "presence"? She replied that she hadn't. In fact she felt whoever, or whatever, it had been, hadn't meant her any harm.

The same thing was to happen every night for the next six weeks. Mrs. Rudge didn't find the experiences very pleasant and she wished whoever it was would go away, but she still didn't feel threatened.

By this time the work on the coach house was nearing completion and the Rudges were preparing to sell their caravan and move into the actual house. One fine bright October morning Mr. and Mrs. Rudge decided to take a rest from all their hard work and go for a walk. They climbed up the steep hill towards the church. They entered the churchyard and slowly walked among the graves. After a time, they decided that it was such a lovely day they'd drive a few kilometres and explore the neighbouring countryside with which they weren't familiar. Mr. Rudge said he'd go back down the hill to the coach house and get out their car. Mrs. Rudge decided to stay by the church for a few moments then join him when he was ready.

Mr. Rudge left the churchyard and set off down the hill. Mrs. Rudge wandered round the church, then, deciding her husband must have the car ready, she started walking away from the church towards the gate.

Suddenly she was almost frightened out of her wits when a hand clamped down on her shoulder. She jumped round in fear to see a lady standing beside her. It was the same lady she'd seen through the caravan windows! This time Mrs. Rudge was horror-struck!

She tore herself away from the grasping hand on her shoulder and ran as fast as she could out of the churchyard and down the hill. Her husband had just got the car started so she leapt into the passenger seat and, babbling like an idiot, told him what had happened.

Mr. Rudge finally managed to calm his wife down but then he, too, had a dreadful shock! He was looking at her coat when he suddenly saw that on the shoulder which the woman's hand had clasped, were pieces of grass and sticky brown mud!

They were both terrified! So much so that they decided to go to the nearest public house and buy a drink to calm their nerves.

They were so shaken by the event that they started telling the landlord what had happened. Strangely enough, neither the landlord nor any of the locals who were listening to the story appeared to be surprised by it! When Mrs. Rudge started to describe the woman, the landlord told her to wait a moment while he went to get something. When he returned he had a small photograph in a frame.

"Is this the woman you saw?" he asked.

"Why yes," replied Mrs. Rudge, "that's her. Without a doubt."

The landlord looked at the locals and they all nodded their heads.

"Who is she?" asked Mr. Rudge.

The landlord replied, "Her name is Emma Vernon. The Vernon family used to be the local landed gentry but this daughter Emma was a bit of a black sheep."

"Was?" said an alarmed Mr. Rudge. "What do you mean by 'was'?"

Calmly, the landlord replied, "She died over a hundred years ago."

The Rudges were now very scared, but they were curious enough to ask what was known about Emma Vernon.

"The story goes that she ran off with the local rector," the landlord explained. "This of course was a great scandal in the neighbourhood, but even more of a scandal was the fact that the rector jilted her and she returned to the village a sad and ruined woman. Unable to bear life any longer she killed herself. This meant that she couldn't be buried inside the churchyard because that was hallowed ground, and she'd committed the dreadful sin of taking her own life. Her grave, therefore, is just outside the churchyard walls."

"But I'll tell you one thing," continued one of the locals, "Emma's grave is all on its own and surrounded by long grass. Nobody ever goes that way and the grass is never cut. But if you go and have a look, you'll see that a clear path has been trodden between her grave and the churchyard gate!"

Mrs. Rudge, although she identified the picture, was adamant that it couldn't have been a ghost she'd met because of the very firm, and extremely life-like, hand that had been clasped on her shoulder.

"Look," she said, and pointed to her shoulder where the bits of grass and mud had been. But there was nothing there! The shoulder of her coat was perfectly clean!

Both Mr. and Mrs. Rudge insisted that they'd seen the earth and grass, but all the locals would do was nod, *knowingly*.

Mrs. Rudge decided to take off her coat and have a closer look at it. As she took it off, her husband cried out in alarm. Mrs. Rudge was wearing a short-sleeved dress—and right across her bare shoulder, where the hand had clasped her, were red finger-nail scratches! *Emma had left her mark after all!!*

THE UNTIDY
SCHOOLBOY

If your school work is rather untidy and your teacher keeps complaining about messy writing and ink blots in your exercise books, then take a lesson from this next ghost story! A long time ago a little boy came to a very nasty end—all because he was untidy in his school work!

Near Marlow, in Berkshire, stands a large Tudor house known as Bisham Abbey. Since 1946 it has belonged to the Central Council of Physical Recreation but many families have owned it over the centuries, the most famous being Henry VIII who gave it to his discarded wife, Anne of Cleves. But the family that are involved in this particular story were called Hoby, and they took possession of the Abbey during the first half of the sixteenth century.

27

Like many old country houses, Bisham Abbey has numerous family portraits hanging on the walls. To this day you can see pictures of the Hoby's in the great hall. One of them is of Lady Elizabeth Hoby, and you can see she has a very white face and hands and is dressed in the black coif, weeds and wimple of a knight's widow. *She* is our ghost!

A few years ago, two boys were returning home late one evening after a day's fishing. As they walked along the river bank at Bisham, one of them stopped and pointed out into the middle of the water. Although it was getting dark and a faint mist was creeping up the river, they could see quite clearly the figure of a woman sitting in a boat. She was old and dressed all in black, and there was no visible reason why she should be sitting there. But the boys knew who she was! She was the ghost of Lady Holby who'd been seen many times wandering through the Abbey symbolically washing her blood-stained hands in a bowl of water that moved before her in mid-air! She has also been heard weeping in the night! She is a very unhappy ghost because she's been left to wander the Abbey for ever, because of her wicked treatment of her son. She was so wicked to him that she actually caused his death!

Here's what happened!

Sir Thomas Holby was a most learned man. He was famous as a scholar and so no-one was surprised when he married Elizabeth, the third daughter of Sir Anthony Cooke, because she shared the general fame of her family for being very clever. Elizabeth was a close friend of Queen Elizabeth and moved in all the best circles. Because she was also a brilliant scholar, (able to write poetry in both Latin and

Greek) she was equally ambitious for her children and determined that they should "get on" in the world. Her one disappointment, therefore, was her youngest son, William. He wasn't bright, he wasn't clever, he was lazy! But worst of all, he was *untidy*. His exercise books were always covered in ink splodges and his words (the ones that weren't crossed out) were badly spelt and hardly legible. Lady Elizabeth was furious with him. At first she tried to talk him into changing his ways, but when his work continued to be very bad and very messy, she started beating him. But the more she beat him the worse he became! Finally he started messing up his work on purpose! What he was hoping to achieve by this, nobody knows, but what he did achieve was to receive harder and harder thrashings, around his head and shoulders.

Some writers say he was beaten so hard that one day his mother actually killed him, but others say his death was far, far, more terrible!

One day, poor William's work was even worse than usual. His mother looked at him in despair and asked him why it was that he was so stupid and dirty. The lad couldn't answer her. Very near to losing her temper, Lady Elizabeth gave him another piece of work to do, this time threatening him with the biggest thrashing of his life if he didn't do it properly! William attempted to do the work, but once again the end result was far from satisfactory. Lady Elizabeth looked at the work then completely lost control of herself. She beat him and thrashed him till the poor lad was barely alive. She then locked him in a cupboard with his "hated" books and told him he wouldn't be released until he had finished his exercises properly.

Then the tragedy happened!

A messenger arrived at Bisham saying that Her Majesty wanted Lady Hoby immediately at court. This was an order that had to be obeyed so Lady Elizabeth left her home in a great hurry, forgetting to mention to the servants that William was locked in the cupboard!

When she arrived at court she became so busy with affairs of state that she completely forgot about her poor son. When she returned to Bisham Abbey sometime later, she discovered her son, still locked in the cupboard, but dead from *starvation!*

For the rest of her life, until she died in 1609 at the age of ninety-one, she never forgave herself for her neglect and cruel treatment. Nor has she forgiven herself in the after-life! Her ghostly figure can still be seen to this day, wandering through the house displaying her agony and grief!

A pathetic sequel to the story happened in 1840 when some building work was being done at the Abbey. As workmen were taking down a sixteenth century window shutter, they discovered some very old exercise books pushed into the wall between the joists and the skirting body. William Hoby's name was written on them and the pages were filled with his untidy writing. The last page of one of the books appeared to be heavily blotted— and smudged with tears!

THE SKELETONS
THAT RIDE

If you've ever been to Norfolk, you'll probably have seen the famous Potter Heigham Bridge. But if I were you I wouldn't go near it on May 31st! Every year, on that date, a dreadful spectacle can be seen that terrifies any unlucky person who's around at the time! This is what happened!

On May 31st, 1742, Sir Godfrey Haslitt married the beautiful Lady Evelyn Crew. Both came from very good families and the wedding was a splendid affair in Norwich Cathedral. But what Sir Godfrey didn't know was that his bride had been so much

31

in love with him that, to make sure she "got" him, she'd made a contract with the devil! It was a dreadful thing to do but she had done it "for the sake of love". Little did she know the terrible price she would have to pay for asking the Devil's help.

The wedding reception had hardly started when the Devil demanded his "price"! On the stroke of midnight, the bride was seized at the hall and carried struggling and screaming to a waiting coach, pulled by four coal-black horses who were stamping and snorting in the night air. The occupants of the coach dragged the terrified girl inside with them, then whipped the horses who raced off down the drive.

The coach thundered down the road towards Potter Heigham Bridge. As the coal-black horses's hooves clattered across the cobbles, the girl's screams ripped into the night air. Not many people were about at that time, but those who were saw a luminous coach racing along the road. It was swaying from side to side, its wheels glowing brightly and sparks flying from them as they sped over the road. Perched high on the driver's seat was the grinning mask of a skeleton!

When the coach arrived at Potter Heigham Bridge it swung across the narrow road and crashed into the centre of the bridge wall. The coach broke into a thousand pieces and they, and the horses, and all the occupants of the coach, were thrown over the parapet and flung into the river Thurne below.

Not one body or one piece of the coach were ever recovered!

Every year, on May 31st, the same coach with its ghastly skeletons can be seen driving over the bridge at midnight! A place to steer clear of!!!

THE BAYING HOUNDS

If you have a pet dog, you probably think of it as a cuddly, affectionate, occasionally naughty, bundle of fun. Some dogs are more obedient than others, but unless they are unusually snappy you probably don't regard them as frightening! But in many parts of the country there are ghostly dogs who appear on dark and gloomy nights and terrify anyone who happens to see them. Here is one such story.

At Galashiels, in Selkirk, you can still see the remains of a once vast building known as Buckholm Tower. Most of the original building is in ruins but one tower is almost complete. At the base of the tower is an entrance which leads you down to the dungeons. They are dark, damp, smelly and cold but, worst of all, you can still see a grisly row of iron hooks hanging from the ceiling, which in olden days were used for the tying up and torturing of prisoners. It is about the use of these revolting hooks that this story is concerned.

A former laird, or lord, of Buckholm was called Pringle. He was a very violent and cruel man, and he ill-treated his wife and son so badly that to save their own lives they ran away. Left on his own, the Laird became a drunkard and used to vent his anger on any poor unfortunate person who happened to cross him.

At that time in Scotland, there were many groups of religious people who were trying to break away from the main body of the established church. Whatever their reason for breaking away, all they wanted was to be left in peace to practise their own religion in their own way. But many people wouldn't leave them alone.

One such man was Laird Pringle. He owned two large ferocious dogs which he kept mainly for tracking down members of these religious groups. Other people chased them because they had strong religious beliefs and felt that these break-away groups were *wrong*, Laird Pringle chased them for *fun*.

The local outlawed religious group was the "Convenanters" and, one day, Pringle heard that a secret meeting was to take place in the forest. He gathered his dogs and set off to catch them in the middle of their meeting. When he arrived, he was absolutely furious to find that they'd been warned of his hunt and most of them had fled. The only ones left behind were an old man called Geordie Elliot, who'd been thrown from his horse and badly hurt, and his son who had stayed on to help him. Pringle wanted to kill the two men on the spot, but just then local troopers arrived and stopped him from carrying out his plan. Instead they persuaded him to take the men back to Buckholm Tower where they could be kept safely overnight in the dungeon, to be collected by the militia in the morning.

At first Pringle didn't want to be bothered with the prisoners, but finally he was persuaded to "help", so tied them up and hurried them through the forest with his snarling dogs snapping at their heels.

Back at the Tower, he threw the old man and the boy into the dungeon then went upstairs to relax after his "exhausting" day's work. He dined well then started drinking. The more he thought about his two prisoners, the more he felt happy! The more he felt happy, the more he drank! His servants, knowing how nasty he'd become after a lot of drinking, all retired early to bed.

Hours later, and many drinks later, everyone in the household was woken by loud cries coming from the direction of the dungeon. The prisoners had been left chained up without food and water, and Pringle had forbidden the servants to go near them. It was now very late at night and the alarmed servants got up and crept downstairs to see what was going on. As the cries from the dungeon grew louder, they suddenly heard a crash from the room where the Laird was still drinking. They then saw Pringle stagger across the hall, shouting and cursing as he went, and practically fall down the dungeon stairs. The servants followed him but stopped outside the door. From inside they could hear the most terrible sounds, but they were too frightened to do anything about it.

Finally the sounds in the dungeon stopped. The

screams and cries had died away into complete silence, but the servants found the silence even more terrifying than the noise!

Suddenly there was a loud banging on the front door. Isobel Elliot had come to look for her husband and son. Pringle opened the front door, then grabbed the woman and dragged her downstairs into the dungeon. The poor woman fell to her knees, screaming, as she saw the bodies of her loved ones hanging from the torture hooks!

She sobbed uncontrollably and then cursed Pringle for what he'd done. She swore that the memory of his evil deeds would pursue him like the hounds of hell and that he'd never have any rest.

From that day onwards, Pringle was convinced that he was being haunted. He thought that ghostly hounds were chasing him night and day! His mind became tortured and he could neither eat nor sleep. Finally, he died a very painful death, convinced to the bitter end that he was being hounded.

Every year since then, on the anniversary of his death in June, witnesses have seen a ghostly figure running screaming from the tower, with baying hounds pursuing it. At the same time, terrible blood-curdling cries can be heard coming from the dungeon. As the figure runs from the hounds, the Laird's voice is heard calling for help, then as quickly as it starts, the noise stops and there is absolute silence—until the following year!

THE WOMAN IN WHITE

*Sailors are said to be very superstitious people! They believe in omens about their voyages and take great care not to break any superstition that might call up an evil spirit. If someone sees a ghost on dry land the easy way **not** to see it again is to leave the haunted place. But on board ship it is impossible to "leave" when the ship is at sea, and when it is moored they also can't leave because it is their place of work. The only thing they can do is give up their job! A very serious step, so the sailors who have done this must have been very frightened indeed by the ghosts they saw. Here is a story about a dreadful ghost known as the "woman in white".*

One night in 1850, the *H.M.S. Asp* was at anchor at Milford Haven, South Wales. In the middle of the night, the Captain was woken by a dreadful banging on his cabin door. The Quarter-Master rushed in saying, "Please come on deck, sir. The look-out man has been to fetch me and seems to be in a terribly shocked state."

The Captain wasn't at all pleased to be woken in the middle of the night, but he got up and made his way to the main deck. There he found his look-out man almost speechless with fright.

"I'm going to die for sure tonight!" he cried hysterically.

Captain Alldridge angrily commanded the man to pull himself together and explain what had happened. Eventually the man was able to tell his story.

"I was at my post, sir," he managed to say, "when all of a sudden this figure appeared before me. At first I could not tell what manner of person it was, but my skin crept, sir. I went cold all over! Then I could see that it was a woman, all in white sir!" At this point the look-out became greatly upset once more and had to be calmed down. "Then sir, this ... this ... woman, who was standing on the paddle box, lifted her arm and pointed at the sky."

The Captain ordered the man to return to his duties and not to be so silly, or he would be flogged in the morning.

The look-out returned to his duties but, as he kept watch, he was suddenly overcome by a terrible fit, and had to be carried below by his mates.

And he wasn't the only one to see the ghost!

One Sunday, the ship was moored in Haverfordwest River, and all the crew had shore leave. The

40

only man left on board was the steward. A very ordinary man with little imagination. He was just coming down a companion ladder, thinking of nothing in particular, when a husky voice spoke to him! He turned round quickly, and although there was no-one there, he felt himself slowly falling backwards. He crashed to the deck at the bottom of the ladder, injuring himself in the fall.

When Captain Alldridge returned on board, the steward told him of the disembodied voice that had spoken to him. At first the Captain was angry, but the man looked dreadful and begged for his immediate discharge from the Navy. The Captain, thinking that the man was in such a state he wouldn't be able to carry out his duties, agreed. The steward immediately rushed off to collect his belongings as he didn't want to spend another minute on the ship. The Captain signed his papers and the man ran off down the gangway.

Gradually more and more seamen reported seeing the ghost. Many of them were so scared that they asked for their discharge papers. The Captain had to let them have them because, if he didn't, they simply ran away.

The strange and terrifying thing was that they all told the *same* story. The figure was always that of a woman dressed in white with her arm pointing up at the sky. The Captain still didn't really believe the stories, until one night!

He was asleep in bed when suddenly he woke up. There was nobody in the room, but he could feel a hand placed on his leg above the bedclothes! The touch was icy, even through the thick woollen blankets, and the cabin had become very cold!

41

The same thing happened again the following night! And again! And again! But the Captain was a brave man so it didn't bother him too much.

At last something happened which really did shake him. Once more he was woken suddenly from his sleep, but this time he could feel a hand stroking his forehead! Afterwards he said that every hair on his head stood up in fright and he had leapt out of bed, but again his cabin was empty!

Now, like all the members of his crew, Captain Alldridge became terrified at the thought of the ghost. Who could it be? What did she want? He started making enquiries to see if anyone knew who the ghost could be? It took him a long time, but finally he found the answer! He wished he hadn't!

The *H.M.S. Asp* was a large sailing vessel capable of carrying a fair number of fee-paying passengers. On one voyage, between Port Patrick and Donaghadee, a dreadful event took place which was the cause of the hauntings for those many years after. At the end of the journey, a stewardess set off round the ship to do her usual duty of checking that all passengers had left their cabins. In one cabin she found a beautiful, dark-haired girl lying on a berth. She was wearing a long white nightdress and the stewardess assumed that she had overslept and not noticed that the ship had arrived in port.

The stewardess went to wake her, but then discovered to her horror that the girl's throat had been cut and she was covered in blood! No-one ever discovered who the girl was, why she had been murdered or who had murdered her. But obviously she couldn't rest in peace and was haunting the ship to find her murderer!

As soon as Captain Alldridge found out the facts, it made the appearance of the ghost even more terrifying! She continued to haunt the ship and the Captain was beginning to despair of keeping a full crew. He also wondered how long the poor tortured creature would continue in her desperate search for her murderer—and what dreadful thing would happen if she found him?

Finally, the ghost made her last appearance.

In 1857, *H.M.S. Asp* was docked in Pembroke for repairs. On the second night, a sentry swore he saw a figure climb onto the paddle box of the ship. He noticed it was the figure of a woman pointing at the sky. The figure then left the ship and moved towards him. The sentry didn't know the story of the ghost, he just knew that no woman had any business being on the ship.

He pointed his musket at the figure and shouted, "Who goes there?" The figure took no notice and continued to advance. It walked straight through the barrel of the musket which the sentry dropped in absolute panic as he ran to the guardhouse. The sentry standing next to him had seen the ghastly sight but was made of sterner stuff and stood his ground. He fired his gun to attract the attention of his Guard Commander.

Further down the quay a third sentry was on guard. He saw the figure of a woman dressed all in white walking towards him. She walked straight past without a glance and made her way to the ruined Pater Old Church which was opposite the dockyard. The sentry, being very courageous, climbed onto a wall to watch. He saw the ghost walk into the disused churchyard and make its way to an old grave. It stood on the mound and pointed up to the sky. Then slowly, very slowly, as if she'd come to the end of her search, but a search which hadn't been successful, the wretched ghost sank gradually into the grave. Slower and slower, lower and lower, until it finally disappeared into the ground!

The ghost never appeared again!

THE GHOSTLY
SHIPWRECK

John Jones couldn't sleep. Outside his small cottage near Moelfre Bay in Anglesey, the wind howled and raged. Forks of lightning flashed through the sky and rolls of thunder echoed across the rocks and rolled around the cliffs. Never in his eighty years had John Jones heard such a storm! It was all the more frightening because he was alone in his cottage. His only son was at sea, and although he wrote to his father as much as possible, most of his trips took him far, far away from Wales.

On that dark October night in 1859, all the villagers prayed for the safety of any mariners who were out in the Irish Sea, but the storm was so bad that most of them feared some ship, somewhere, would be wrecked on the cruel rocks around the coast.

When he was a young man, John Jones loved storms. Many a night he would climb along the cliff paths, battling against the wind, to watch the waves crashing against the rocks.

Strange to say, on this most dreadful night, despite his age, he felt a strong urge to go outside and watch the storm. By the light of his candle he put on as many warm clothes as he could find, then, wrapping a shawl around his shoulders, he struggled to open the cottage door. The wind was so strong that he had to put all his weight against it to get it open. It was even more difficult to close behind him.

The power of the wind almost took his breath away, and the thought of climbing up the steep cliff path nearly made him rush back inside.

But something made him go on.

He was a tough old man and amazingly fit for his age, but he still found the walk up the path more difficult than ever before. Finally he reached a point on top of the cliff and stopped. With difficulty he managed to keep his balance against the tearing gale and, with fascinated horror, he watched enormous waves, travelling at incredible speeds, crashing and smashing against the rocks and cliff wall. Never had he seen such a storm!

Suddenly he heard a sound! Above the awful roar of the wind and waves, he heard the sound that strikes terror into any seaman's heart. The sound of a ship's timbers splintering on rocks. Added to that cracking, rending noise, he could soon hear the piteous cries, shouts and wails of human beings in distress. How dreadful!

All of a sudden, the storm seemed to die down and a gloriously bright moon came out from behind dark clouds. But John Jones wished the moon hadn't appeared because, by its bright light, he could see the whole wretched drama unfolding before his eyes. Way down below him at the foot of the cliffs he could see, perfectly clearly, a large, fully-rigged steamship smashed to pieces against the treacherous Moelfre rocks.

Around the wreck people were struggling in the waves. There looked like hundreds of them. John Jones wanted to close his ears to their terrible screaming.

Suddenly, the old man saw a figure struggling through the water who looked familiar. "Oh my God," he cried, "it's my son!" Then, above the sound of the waves and the wind, he heard clearly the one voice he loved more than any other. His only son shouted back from the waves, "My father! My father!" Then John Jones's son disappeared under the foaming waters!

John Jones stood still, rigid with fear. Could he have been mistaken? His son was supposed to be on the other side of the world. But then he heard again the unmistakable voice, and he knew he'd just seen his son being swallowed by the cruel sea. And, as he watched, he also saw the proud ship being engulfed by the merciless waves. As it went down he could clearly read the words *Royal Charter* on its side.

How he got home he never knew. Tears blinded his eyes as he half stumbled, half crawled, back down the steep cliff path. Finally he reached his home. His strength failing, he managed to open the cottage door and stagger inside. He collapsed in his chair.

But then he remembered, his son wasn't on the

47

Royal Charter. His son was in a completely different part of the world on a completely different ship. Perhaps he'd imagined the whole thing? He was an old man after all, perhaps his mind was playing tricks with him. John Jones went to bed and slept fairly well until the morning.

But he hadn't imagined it.

Next morning the shocking news broke over Britain that the magnificent *Royal Charter* had been shipwrecked on the Moelfre rocks with the loss of four hundred and thirty lives. One week later he received a message from the owners of the *Royal Charter* condoling him on the loss of his son by drowning. John Jones's son had transferred to the ship in order to get home on leave a few weeks earlier than he had told his father in his last letter.

John Jones lived for just one year after the news of his son's death. He never got over the tragic loss, or the sight of the wreck on the rocks beneath him. But there was one thing about the whole incident that could never be explained. From where John Jones had been standing on the cliff, he could not possibly have seen the wreck! Nor could he have seen his son drown! Because the *Royal Charter* had gone down on the other side of the rock, *completely out of his view*!

THE HIDDEN BODY

Chambercombe Manor near Ilfracombe, in Devon, is haunted by the ghost of a tall, smiling lady dressed in grey. Many visitors to the house have seen her and others have heard strange noises and seen objects move about. It is the ghost of Kate Oatway who died a violent death, but what is even more horrid is what was done to her body!

A hundred and fifty years ago, the Manor was occupied by a perfectly ordinary farmer and his wife. One day the wife was going to market and she asked her husband to do some repairs to the thatched roof. He wasn't terribly keen on the idea but did look at the roof to see how much work needed to be done. As he peered up, he suddenly

49

found the outline of a window that he'd never noticed before. He leant a ladder against the wall and climbed up to have a look. Sure enough, there was the sill and there was a bricked-in window. Very puzzled, he counted the other windows along that wall and, as he expected, they matched the number of rooms in the house. So which room did this window belong to?

He decided to explore further. He went into the house and started examining an interior wall that he estimated should be very near to the mysterious window. Soon he realised that there must be a hidden room. Just then his wife returned from the market and together they broke down the interior wall. Sure enough, behind the wall was a small room which they'd never known existed.

Rather nervously, they climbed through the hole they'd made and started examining the room. It was fully furnished and decorated, but covered in thick layers of dust. In the middle of the room was a four-poster bed surrounded by faded and mouldy tapestries. The farmer stepped forward and nervously started to pull back the tapestry curtain. Suddenly, the material completely crumbled and dropped to the floor in a cloud of dust. The couple sprang back in horror at what they saw.

Lying on the bed was a skeleton! Complete, white and shining!

If you visit Chambercombe Manor today, you can see the hidden room, which kept its dreadful secret for many hundreds of years. You can also discover the truth behind the ghostly hauntings by Kate Oatway, because it was her body that was bricked up in that room.

That part of the Devon coastline is dangerously rocky and, in olden days, was very treacherous for passing ships. Many were the wrecks washed up along the shore, which, although very unfortunate for the crew, passengers and ship owners, was very fortunate for the locals because of the booty they could steal from the wrecked hulls. To make matters worse, certain wicked men used to play tricks with lights, so that unsuspecting captains would be fooled into thinking they were sailing into a safe harbour, when really they were being led straight onto the rocks.

One such man, who was well-known for his wrecking tricks, was a gentleman called Alexander Oatway. He was a rich landowner who, at the time of this story, was living in Chambercombe Manor. One stormy night, when the wrecking "lights" had lured yet another ship onto the rocks, "Wrecker" Oatway, as he was called, joined his band of helpers on the beach to see what they could salvage. What he didn't know was that his seventeen year old son, William, had become suspicious of his father's activities and had followed him down to the shore. As he stood on the beach, horrified by the sight of the wrecked ship and his father's actions, he suddenly heard a voice crying out for help. Scrambling over the rocks he came across a half-conscious girl. He carried her back up to the Manor and nursed her back to health.

"Wrecker" Oatway was very angry! This Spanish girl, who had been washed overboard from the wreck, was an eye witness to his evil deeds. He swore the girl to secrecy then gave up his ownership of the Manor and moved to Plymouth. He sent his son to Tavistock to keep him out of the way.

William became a successful businessman then, one day, he met the Spanish girl again at a dance. They fell in love and, shortly afterwards, married. Although he enjoyed living and working in Tavistock, his ambition was to return to Chambercombe Manor. He couldn't afford to buy it, but when he heard it was vacant, he eagerly took up the tenancy.

By this time he had a lovely daughter called Kate and, as the years went by, she became even more beautiful.

One day she met an Irishman called Wallace, who was the Captain of a pirate ship. They fell in love and, when they were married, Wallace took her off to his home in Dublin. She was very sorry to leave her parents, but promised that one day she would come back and visit them.

The years passed happily for William Oatway and his wife although he never raised enough money to buy the Manor. There continued to be wrecks along the coast, but William was a law-abiding man whose only interest in the ships was, if he could, to help the captains and their passengers.

One stormy night he went down onto the beach as usual to see if there were any ships in distress, and for the second time in his life he heard a cry for help. Scrambling over the rocks he once more found the body of a young woman. But this time the woman was in a very bad state, as she'd been bashed and thrown savagely against the rocks by the enormous waves. William took her up to the Manor but she died that night. As he and his wife prepared her body for burial they discovered a money belt strapped around her waist. Unable to help himself, William saw that here were enough jewels and gold coins to enable him to buy his beloved Manor, so he took the belt off the body.

The next day a shipping agent called at the Manor to see if they knew anything of a missing passenger off the wrecked ship. William, thinking about the money belt he'd stolen, denied all knowledge of the woman. But when he heard the woman's name he was overcome with horror and grief. Filled with shame, he walled up her body in the secret room then left the Manor never to return.

The name of the woman passenger had been *Mrs. Katherine Wallace!* He'd robbed the dead body of his own daughter, Kate!

It's no wonder that Kate Oatway haunts the Manor where her own father had comitted such a dreadful deed!

NO. 50
BERKELEY SQUARE

In the centre of London there is a very wealthy and fashionable district called Mayfair. In one area, known as Berkeley square, there is an ordinary looking four-storey building which is now used as an office for a well known firm of booksellers. There are three windows on the top three floors and two windows and a door on the ground floor. The address? 50 Berkeley Square!

When tourists visit London they are usually directed to the Houses of Parliament; Buckingham Palace; the Tower of London and other such famous places. But during the reign of Queen Victoria, very high on the list of places to visit was a building in Berkeley Square. Hundreds of visitors would make a special journey to stand outside number 50 Berkeley Square and stare at its chipped and peeling paintwork. Why? Because No. 50 Berkeley Square had experienced so many horrific and terrifying ghostly "happenings" that the whole place was deserted.

Nobody had the courage to live there, because at least two people had been frightened to death and others experienced appalling, nameless horrors!

Here are some of the stories connected with this ghastly, ghostly, building!

*   *   *

"Where are you going?"

The old servant stopped at the foot of the stairs and turned to see who had spoken. Standing in the doorway to the servant's hall was the new butler.

"I'm just delivering the supper," the old man replied.

The young man moved from the shadows of the doorway and approached the stairs.

"What supper?" he asked.

The old man looked at him with wide eyes. He didn't know what to say.

"I asked you a question," said the young man coldly. "What supper?"

The new butler had only joined the household that morning. He was a young man of unsettled background who'd never been able to keep a job for longer than a few months. His parents had "given up" with him many years before when they saw him jumping from one scrape to the next. The only member of the family who had time for him was his Aunt Sophie. She was a solid respectable woman who always found room in her heart to forgive her rakish nephew his wild excesses. For some months she'd been employed as a cook at 50 Berkeley Square by a Mr. du Pré of Wilton Park. It wasn't the happiest of employment because all the other servants seemed to come and go by the week, but as she was only concerned with the cooking, she didn't bother herself with what went on in the rest of the house. So when her young nephew arrived, once again to see his favourite aunt after yet another scrape, she decided to get him a proper job in her own household. To be honest, he wasn't too keen on the idea as he hated the thought of being tied down, but when the butler gave in his notice (he'd only been there two weeks) and his aunt assured her nephew he could get the position, he decided to give it a go!

To his surprise, but not his conceit, the housekeeper was only too pleased to find a young man prepared to take on the position. When he asked his aunt why the servants kept handing in their notice, all she did was shrug and tell him to get on with the job and not poke his nose into other people's affairs! She gave him a quick lesson in what to do, and what not to do as a butler, and he started his duties.

"I asked you a question. What supper?"

The old servant licked his lips nervously.

The new butler had seen this old man skulking around the kitchen. He didn't really know what his job was, nor did he have the humility to ask, he just waited until he caught him doing something that looked odd. As far as he knew, the delivering of meals was the job of the footman or the upstairs maid, not a ragged old scullery manservant.

The old servant clutched the tray he was carrying, coughed, then whispered in the young man's ear.

"You don't know then?"

"Know what?" the young man replied.

The old man shook his head. "I shouldn't ask if I were you. There are things in this house that a young man shouldn't know about."

The old man turned and carried on up the stairs, leaving the new butler looking after him in astonishment.

Later, in the kitchen, the young man asked his aunt about the old man's job of delivering a meal tray. Aunt Sophie looked at him. "Every night I prepare a tray of cold meat, bread and water. I leave it on the scullery table at half past five and the next morning it's empty."

"Where does it go?" asked her nephew.

The cook shook her head. "I don't know, and I don't ask. If you're sensible you won't ask either."

But that wasn't enough for this adventurous young man. The next night he waited outside the scullery until he heard the tray being picked up. He heard footsteps moving away, then started after them. Entering the hall, he saw the old manservant walking up the stairs. He followed. The old man carried the tray up to the third floor—the young man had never been on this floor—walked to the far end of the corridor, then bent down and put the tray on the floor outside a solid-looking door. The young butler crept forward in the shadows. Then he heard a sickening sound!

It wasn't exactly a cry, or even a scream, or even a groan! More like an animal in pain—but also frightened and angry!

The young butler watched the old man lean for-ward and take hold of some sort of handle on the door. Quickly, the old man's arm moved sideways and a shaft of light shot across the floor of the corridor. Equally as quickly, the contents of the tray were thrown into the light, then slam, and the light had gone!

The young man pressed himself into a corner as the old man shuffled past him carrying the, now empty, tray. As he waited in the shadows, all he could hear were the footsteps of the old man, plus a gobbling, revolting sound coming from the other side of the heavy door. Then there was silence—followed by a banging and crashing and tearing sound, like he'd never heard before! Or ever wished to hear again!

Did that really happen at No. 50 Berkeley Square? Who knows? But one story is that Mr. du Pré kept his insane brother locked in an upstairs room. He was so violent that no-one could handle him so he had to be fed through a special opening in the door. Many people believe it is the mad brother who haunts the building! But there are other stories!

*   *   *

In December 1887, the frigate *Penelope* docked in Portsmouth. Two sailors, Edward Blunden and Robert Martin set off for their homes. They arrived in London on Christmas Eve with very little money in their pockets and nowhere to stay for the night. They wandered the streets until they saw a "TO LET" sign outside a empty house. No. 50 Berkeley Square!

59

They weren't worried about entering a deserted house and managed to get in through a window in the basement. It was pitch black, but one of them had a candle so they could pick their way through the rooms. By the light of the candle, they could see that the whole house had been left to rack and ruin. Broken furniture, piles of rubbish, scattered objects and piles of dust were everywhere. Even rats!

The basement was very unpleasant so they decided to explore the ground floor. Again, all they found was rubbish and discarded furniture. Wanting to find a reasonable room where they could spend the night, they pressed onwards and upwards to the first floor. The candle was beginning to flicker, and Edward Blunden's courage flickered with it, but Robert Martin forced him to climb higher to the second floor.

"I don't like this much," said Blunden.

"Don't be stupid," replied Martin. "Why should we pay for a night's lodgings when this place is free?" Martin looked around him at the dirt and dust. "I know it ain't much, but at least it's dry and warm for a few hours."

By this time Blunden was feeling very nervous but Martin pushed him into a bedroom. What they didn't know was that this was the so-called "haunted room". *The reason why the house had been deserted for forty years!*

The room seemed to be less disordered than the others and the two sailors felt that they could sort out reasonable beds for the night. The fire-place didn't look too cluttered so they set fire to odd bits of wood. Feeling reasonably comfortable and warm, Martin went straight to sleep. But Blunden felt uneasy, and it was he who first heard the noises!

They sounded like footsteps—*but not normal footsteps!*

"Listen!" Blunden tugged at Martin's clothes.

"What?" Martin struggled awake. Then he too heard the noises!

The sound of a shoe on wood, or a shoe on stone—that is easy to explain, but the sound that Martin and Blunden heard wasn't like either of these! The steps were soft, but there was also a scratching sound—just like an animal's claws or a bird's talons. Martin and Blunden looked at each other in terror. Whatever was walking up the stairs and towards their room, certainly wasn't human!

The steps came nearer and nearer. Were they going to go past? No! The door slowly opened and a figure stepped in. But what a figure! A whiteish, shapeless form that seemed to grow larger as they watched! The two men leapt to their feet in horror.

Blunden looked round for something he could use to protect himself. He saw an old piece of curtain rod leaning against a wall, so he rushed across the room and grabbed it. This action seemed to attract the attention of the ghostly spectre, and it turned towards him. It then began to move across the floor towards Blunden and, as it did so, two arms appeared from its shapeless body. But not like real arms, more like a huge bird's talons! Blunden screamed as the figure came nearer and nearer.

Martin, frightened almost out of his mind, didn't wait to see what happened to his friend because he could see the door was now unguarded. He dived towards it, raced along the landing and threw himself down the stairs. Screaming with fear he tore open the huge front door and raced out into the street, running wildly from the square until he finally bumped into a policeman in Piccadilly.

"Help," he managed to gasp. "Come and help!"

He pulled the policeman back to Berkeley Square and pointed to the house. "My mate and I were just kipping there. We didn't mean no harm. Now he's up there alone. . . . with. . : ."

"Good God!" muttered the policeman. "You ain't been in there?"

Together they ran to where the glow from a gas lamp showed the "TO LET" sign outside the open door of No. 50 Berkeley Square. Suddenly there was a crash of glass, the splintering of wood, a wild scream. Then silence.

They found the shattered body of Blunden draped over the steps below the first floor window, *his eyes still wide with fear!*

Nobody could offer an explanation as to what it was that had frightened Blunden to death! Nor could anyone explain this next terrifying "happening" at No. 50 Berkeley Square.

*　　*　　*

Sir Robert Worboys was a handsome young man-about-town with an ancestral home at Bracknell, in Berkshire. He was a very solid young man who dismissed the idea of ghosts or supernatural happenings as "pure imagination".

One day at his club, White's, the subject of No. 50 Berkeley Square was raised in conversation, and Sir Robert scoffed at all the stories about the place.

"Rubbish, my dear friends!" he scoffed. "The

whole thing is nonsense. If these people came to an untimely death when living, or staying in the house, then it was probably their own fault. People can be remarkably clumsy you know."

His friends insisted that the stories were true, but Sir Robert simply laughed. Finally his friends bet him that he wouldn't spend a night in the haunted room, to which, merrily, Sir Robert agreed.

"You'll only lose your money," he laughed.

A friend, Lord Cholmondeley, introduced Sir Robert to the owner of 50 Berkeley Square, Mr. Benson. Mr. Benson didn't think the idea of Sir Robert staying in the house was at all funny.

"Come, come Mr. Benson," chided Sir Robert. "Your reluctance to talk about the matter must be because you think the idea of ghosts is nonsense as well."

"Not at all, Sir Robert," replied Benson. "The hauntings at No. 50 are so well-known that I do not doubt the existence of a supernatural agent."

"Well, let me spend one night there, and I'll prove the whole thing is nonsense."

Mr. Benson wasn't happy. He knew very well what had happened to other people in the house and this idea of a bet was not to his liking. But after a great deal of persuasion from Sir Robert and his friends, he finally gave in—under certain conditions. Sir Robert would be armed, he would ring for help if he should find himself in trouble, and his friends would stay the night on the floor below. This was agreed.

The night for the adventure arrived. The entire party met at Mr. Benson's house for a meal. They were all nervous, but trying to hide the fact. All, that is, except Mr. Benson, who once again tried to dissuade Sir Robert.

"Afraid not Mr. Benson, it's now a matter of honour." But even Sir Robert was becoming nervous. "I think the best thing gentlemen, in case my excitement leads me to ring the bell without very good reason, is for you to wait until I ring the bell twice — if I ring it at all," he added. He could not be persuaded to change his mind.

All the arrangements were discussed yet again, then Sir Robert was shown to the room. It was a large and comfortably furnished room with a double bed and armchairs. There was a fire in the grate and two windows looking out over the Square. At a quarter past eleven he lay down on the bed, one hand close to his pistol, the other near the bell-pull. One flight below, in the drawing room, Mr. Benson, Lord Cholmondeley and the other friends settled down for the night.

At midnight, the bell in the drawing room rang once. Mr. Benson shot out of his chair and ran to the door. One of the others cried out, "Wait! He said he would ring twice if he needed us."

He had hardly finished speaking when the bell started ringing loudly and violently. All the men in the room rushed out of the door and up the stairs. Halfway up they heard the sound of a shot coming from the haunted room. As soon as they reached the landing, Mr. Benson was the first to open the door. Inside they found Sir Robert lying across the bed, his head hanging over the edge almost touching the floor. In his left hand was the bell pull, which had torn away from the wall, and on the floor near his right hand was the pistol. He was dead. Someone looked at his face. "My God!" he cried out. "Cover him up." Sir Robert's eyes were wide open and bulging in fear, and his lips were curled back over his tightly-clenched teeth. He hadn't been shot—he had died of fear!

Would *you* like to go and visit 50 Berkeley Square?

POWYS CASTLE

Nobody would describe Powys Castle in North Wales as an attractive building. In fact it's pretty ugly! It stands high up on a rock in the middle of a well-wooded park, the only thing to attract your attention being its red-coloured stone work, which explains its nickname Castell Coch or Red Castle. The only other thing that might attract you to Powys Castle is the story of its ghost!

In 1780 there lived a poor young woman called Jenny Thomas, who made her living by visiting all the big houses in the area to do their spinning. It was the custom for the householder to give Jenny her meals, a bed for the night and a small present when she'd finished the work.

One day she arrived at Powys Castle to do a couple of days' work. The family were staying in their home in London, but the steward and his wife made all the necessary arrangements for Jenny's stay in the house. When it was time to go to bed, three of the servants, each carrying a lighted candle, showed her to her room. It was a very spacious apartment on the ground floor with handsome furniture, in fact it was so grand that Jenny was surprised she should be allowed to sleep in it! There was a blazing fire in the hearth and the servants had put a table and chair in front of it for her to do her work. They told her she could go to bed whenever she wanted, then the three servants left the room pulling the door tightly shut behind them. Jenny looked round happily at the room, thoroughly enjoying this rare bit of luxury, then she settled down at the table to read her Bible—a thing she did every night before saying her prayers and going to bed.

As she was reading, she suddenly saw the candle flame flicker and felt a draught. Turning her head, she was astonished to see the door open and a man walk into her room. He was very fashionably dressed and wearing a three-cornered hat edged with gold lace.

Jenny jumped up and bobbed him a curtsey because he was obviously a gentleman.

"I am sorry sir," she said, "but this is the servants' wing. Are you lost?"

But the man didn't reply. Instead he walked to one of the windows and leant his elbow on the sill, his face resting in the palm of his hand. He stayed there for some time without moving. Jenny looked at him closely to see if she could recognise him, because over the years she had come to know most of the family of the house and their staff. But she'd never seen him before in her life.

Finally he stood up straight, walked back out of the door, without saying a word, and firmly closed the door behind him.

Jenny was alarmed! Who was this strange man? Could he be a ghost? Jenny quickly knelt down by the side of the bed and started saying her prayers. Suddenly the door opened again and once more the man walked into the room. Still without speaking, he moved to stand behind her. Poor Jenny's heart was thumping with fear and she struggled to make a sound—but her lips were too frozen to speak. Then, without warning, the man walked round the room and back out of the door. Again he shut it firmly behind him.

Poor Jenny was trembling with fright, and although she kept telling herself that ghosts walk *through* doors, they don't bother to *open* them, she still felt sure her visitor was a ghost. She prayed that God would give her strength to cope with the situation and, as she began to calm down, she decided that if the "man" came again, she would control her fear and try to speak to him.

She was given the chance!

Still while she was on her knees, she heard the door open for a third time. As before, the man entered the room and walked to stand behind her. She plucked up her courage and spoke.

"Pray, sir, who are you and what do you want?"

The apparition lifted one finger and said, "Take up the candle and follow me, and I will tell you."

Jenny suddenly found that she had lost all control over herself. She found herself standing up, picking up the candle and following him out the door. She couldn't have stopped her actions even if she'd wanted to, she just *had* to obey him.

He led her along a corridor, then stopped outside a door. He opened it and Jenny could see it led to a very small room, rather like a large cupboard. She stopped.

"Walk in," he commanded. "I will not hurt you."

Jenny found herself walking into the room.

"Observe what I do," ordered the ghost, to which Jenny replied, "I will".

Fascinated, Jenny watched him stoop down and start heaving up the floorboards. When the gap was large enough, she could see a box with an iron handle in the lid.

"Do you see that box?" asked the ghost.

"Yes I do," she replied.

He then moved to the far side of the room and showed her a crevice with a key hidden in it.

"This box and key must be taken to the Earl of Powys at his home in London," said the ghost. "Will you see it done?"

Jenny nodded. "I will do my best to get it done."

The ghost replied, "Do so, and I will trouble the house no more."

He then turned and walked straight out through the wall of the room!

Jenny stood in the centre of the room, shocked and amazed. After she'd recovered, and was sure that the apparition had gone, she ran to the door and shouted at the top of her voice.

In the servants' quarters, the steward and his wife were terrified when they heard her cry. For many months, anyone who had stayed in Jenny's room had been greatly disturbed during the night. But when Jenny turned up, because they knew she was a serious-minded woman with great religious belief, they thought they'd put her in the room to see if she could discourage the disturbing influence. When they heard her call, they feared the worst! Picking up lighted candles and calling for all the other servants, they slowly made their way to the room where Jenny was waiting. Afraid that they'd done a dreadful thing by putting her in the "haunted room" they were greatly relieved to find her perfectly all right.

Jenny told them what had happened and showed them the box and the key. The steward was too frightened to do anything but his wife was made of sterner stuff, and made the other servants help her lift the box out of the hole. She then told Jenny that the box and the key would immediately be sent to the Earl in London.

Jenny returned to her bedroom and slept peacefully until morning.

When the Earl opened the box he found it contained priceless jewels and gold coins. As soon as he had been told what had happened, he offered Jenny a home in his house for as long as she wanted. Jenny gratefully accepted the offer and spent the rest of her life under the care of the Earl. But even though she was happy and contented, her one regret was that she never discovered who her "ghost" had been, or why "he" had done what he did? The Earl never found out either!

GLAMIS CASTLE

Glamis Castle in Scotland is an enormous and impressive building. Anybody who is a sincere ghost hunter must certainly include this on their list of places to visit because even on sunny days it looks like a building that hides deep and fearful secrets!

If you go inside Glamis Castle, if you're brave enough, you're even shown proof of some of the dreadful deeds. In one of the rooms you can see a sword and a shirt of mail that belonged to Macbeth, because it was in this room, in AD 1040, that he murdered Duncan. In another room is a special floorboard. It was put down to cover the original floor because when King Malcolm II was killed

73

there, his blood splashed everywhere, and no matter how many times the floor was scrubbed, no-one could remove the stains. The stains are said to be there still!

But the most famous room of all, the "Haunted Room", you cannot enter because no-one knows where it is. So many dreadful things are said to have happened in that room that eventually the owner of the Castle, Lord Strathmore, had the entrance bricked in. Now no-one can find it! A few years ago a party of schoolboys visited the Castle to try to find the room. They visited every room they could find and hung a towel out of each window to show where it was. They were sure they had been into every single room but when they met outside they could see seven windows without a towel hanging from them!

There are so many horrible stories about the "Haunted Room" that we've devoted two whole chapters to telling them. We were so frightened by them that we suggest you only read these stories in a room with *all* the lights on!!

GLAMIS CASTLE
—1—
A CARD GAME
WITH THE DEVIL

Many many years ago, Glamis Castle was owned by a very nasty man. The Earl of Strathmore was known by his servants and the local peasants as "Earl Patie". He was famous throughout the area for his heavy drinking, his vile temper and his dreadful language which he shouted at the top of his voice as he stormed around the castle. He was also famous for his love of gambling.

At that time in Scotland, the Lord's Day, Sunday, was kept as a special day when everyone was supposed to rest and spend their time quietly at home. But not Earl Patie!

It all happened on a dark and stormy November night. Earl Patie was bored and fed up with having to stay indoors all day. He wanted to be out riding across the heath but had been forced to stay at home to observe the Sabbath. Finally he could bear it no longer and, swearing loudly, he demanded that his servants bring him a pack of cards. Comforted that he was about to enjoy a pleasant game, he looked around for others to join him at the table. But no-one would play! The ladies were in the chapel praying so he called the servants, one by one, and asked them to play a hand. But none of them would! Even if the wicked *Earl* was prepared to abuse the Lord's Day, none of his *servants* were willing to break the Church's rules. From the steward to the lowest scullery lad, they all made excuses why they couldn't play. Many of them had been forced to play with him on other occasions to prevent him losing his temper, but on this particular day they all found a reason why they had to be somewhere else.

The more the Earl listened to their stories, the angrier he became. He started cursing at them, but it was no good, he couldn't find a partner. In desperation he called on the chaplain to join him but this good man was furious at the suggestion. Pointing at the cards he called them "devil's bricks" and said that dreadful things would happen to anyone who used them on a Sunday.

The Earl swore loudly! He grabbed a pack of cards and, growling to himself, he climbed the old oak stairs to his room. Turning at the top of the stairs he yelled, "I'll play with the Devil himself, rather than be stopped doing what *I* want to do." Then he stamped down the corridor.

Little did he know what was waiting for him!

A few moments later, he was sitting in his room when he heard a knock on the door.

"Do you want a partner?" sounded a deep voice from the corridor.

"Yes!" roared the Earl. "Enter, in the foul fiend's name, whoever you are!"

The door opened, and a tall dark stranger entered the room. He was completely wrapped in a cloak. He nodded in a familiar manner to the Earl, then sat in a vacant chair on the opposite side of the table.

The Earl stared at his strange guest and with a shudder remembered his words at the top of the stairs. "I'll play with the devil himself." But when he looked at the familiar sight of the cards on the table his nervousness vanished. The stranger, who didn't take off his hood and cloak, suggested that they play for a high stake.

The Earl nodded eagerly. "If I lose," he added, "and haven't got the money to pay you, I'll sign my name to a bond which will give you anything you like that belongs to me."

The stranger nodded. The Earl immediately signed a piece of paper and they started to play.

The game became fast and furious. The Earl won the first hand and bellowed with delight, but then the stranger won and the Earl swore and banged the table. So the game continued, first one, then the other winning the hands. The Earl continued yelling and cursing but he wasn't the only one making a noise. As loud as he shouted and swore, the stranger shouted louder!

As the night grew darker and colder, the noise from the Earl's room became louder and more horrific. All the servants huddled at the bottom of the

77

stairs listening to the dreadful noise with their eyes wide open in fear. They asked each other questions in hushed and frightened voices.

"Who is the stranger?"

"Who is it that dares to shout back at the Earl?"

"Will anything happen to them for playing cards on a Sunday?"

They got no answers to their questions just more and more noise from upstairs!

Finally, despite their fears, their curiosity got the better of them and they crept upstairs. As they approached the room the cursing and yelling grew louder and terrifyingly fierce. Keeping close to the walls, they slowly advanced down the long dark corridor. When they reached the room, the butler tiptoed to the door and bending down he peeped through the key-hole.

Then it happened!

With a scream of agony that resounded to the furthest part of the castle, the butler shot backwards from the door. He crashed to the ground and rolled around, screaming at the top of his voice!

Instantly, the door was thrown open and the Earl stormed out—his face black with fury.

"Slay anyone who passes this way," he shouted, then slammed back into the room.

But when the Earl re-entered the room he found it was empty! He searched everywhere, but the stranger was nowhere to be seen—neither was the paper he'd signed at the beginning of their game.

When he was sure the room was completely empty, he rejoined his servants who were huddled round the body of the butler. Frightened by what he might see, the Earl bent down to look at the old man. As soon as he saw his face, he started back in horror. The butler was covered with bruises and round the eye that had looked through the key-hole, was a deep, burnt in, yellow circle.

Slowly the Earl told the servants what had happened. They listened, struck dumb with terror.

"As we sat playing," said the Earl, "the stranger suddenly threw down his cards and said with an-oath, "smite that eye". Immediately a sheet of flame shot straight to the key-hole. That is what hit the butler."

For the first time in his life, the Earl was scared. He knew now who the stranger had been—the Devil! He also realised that he had signed away his soul!

It was five years before the Devil made him pay for his bond, but during those years the Earl was a changed man. Always nervous, frightened of the dark, he lived like a man under sentence of death.

After his death, every Sunday during the month of November, the Earl's old room was filled with the sounds of cursing, yelling and playing of cards. For many years, witnesses who heard the noise said that it sounded as though the Earl was once more playing the Devil to try and win back his soul—but he never succeeded!

GLAMIS CASTLE
—2—
THE HAUNTED ROOM

One night, not so many years ago, Lord Strath-more was entertaining some friends at Glamis Castle. They were relaxing happily after an excellent evening meal, when the noise began. For the guests who had never been to the castle before it was a frightening experience, but the castle's owner and the rest weren't particularly surprised. They didn't like it, but they were able to control their fear.

"What on earth is it?" cried out one guest.

"Just the ghost," replied the Lord.

"I've never heard anything like it," whispered another.

"My friends," said the Lord, "this castle has been besieged by ghosts for hundreds and hundreds of years. In all parts of the castle, people have witnessed ghastly apparitions. There is a tongueless woman who runs across the park, pointing in anguish to her wounded mouth. There's "Jack the Runner" whose strange, thin figure races up the long drive to the castle. A madman walks a certain portion of the roof on stormy nights and a woman with mournful eyes and a pale face peers out of an upper lattice window, her hands clutching at the panes."

The new guests shuffled uncomfortably in their seats, and all the time the Lord talked, the ghostly noises echoed round the room.

"We've even got a witch," said Lord Strathmore. "Well, the ghost of one. Many people have seen a female figure hovering above the clock tower surrounded by a reddish glow. She's said to be a Lady Glamis who was burned to death on Castle Hill, Edinburgh, charged with witchcraft."

One of the guests was disturbed by the ghost stories but he was even more upset by the noise.

"I don't believe in any of that nonsense," he said, "but that infernal din is another matter. Have you got some workmen in?"

The men stopped talking and listened carefully to the noise.

As it boomed around the room it did, for a moment, sound like workmen hammering and banging, but then the noise changed. It was hard to describe exactly what it was, but all the listeners soon felt that it wasn't an earthly sound. Never had they heard anything like it before—and none of them wished to hear it again! It was a mixture of human sounds and unnatural clanks, booms and thumps. There was also a thread of wind and whistling noises mixed in with the rest. Altogether it made their hair stand on end.

Lord Strathmore shook his head, "No. I have no workmen in. That particular sound comes from one room, and I know that there is no-one in there because the door is locked and I have the key. Also, there are only three people who know where that room is, myself, my heir and my factor."

"So what is making that awful noise?" asked one man, his voice shaking with fear.

"I don't know," replied the Lord, "and neither does anyone else. There are many ghastly stories about what has happened in that room, which is why it is locked up." He looked at his guests, "Do you want to hear one of the stories?"

His guests were feeling very uneasy, but they nodded for their host to continue. He did.

"In olden days there were many feuds between rival clans. The Ogilvies and the Lindsays in particular were always fighting. One day, a number of the Ogilvie clan were fleeing for their lives from a battle and coming to Glamis Castle they begged the owner to let them in. He didn't want to refuse them the shelter of his castle walls, but he also didn't really want to let them in. He told them he would hide them, and put them in a large out-of-the-way chamber." Lord Strathmore paused. His guests gulped nervously. Lord Strathmore continued. "He locked them in—and left them there to starve. According to the legend, their bones lie there to this day. Their bodies haven't been removed."

The guests looked at each other without saying a word. If they'd been anywhere else they'd have laughed, but sitting in Glamis Castle, their ears filled with terrifying ghostly sounds, no-one felt like laughing. But one man did feel brave.

"That's just another old tale to frighten your guests," he said cheerfully. "You can't possibly believe it?"

Lord Strathmore shrugged. Some of the other guests also shrugged, but none of them were quite sure what they believed.

"If you don't know," continued the brave man, "why don't you have a look?"

Throughout his life, Lord Strathmore had known the awful stories about his home. He'd grown up with the noises and he'd learnt to live with his fear. But never once had he looked in the "Haunted Room". Guests had been woken in the night by strange apparitions floating through their bedrooms; others had fled from the castle terrified by nameless sights; many a night he'd been too frightened to close his eyes for sleep in case he was woken by something dreadful. But did he have the courage to find out more about the ghosts? If he entered the Haunted Room what would he really find?

Lord Strathmore looked at his guests, then slowly rising from his seat he said, "Very well! Let us go and open the door. All of you who are brave enough to face the Haunted Room, and whatever nameless horrors we may find, come with me".

The Lord left the room. His guests looked at each other nervously. The last thing that most of them wanted to do was to explore the Haunted Room, but if they stayed behind they knew that they'd be called "cowards", so they all quietly followed their host.

As they entered the hall they saw Lord Strathmore waiting for them at the top of the stairs. His face was white and his body stiff with fear of what they were about to do. Without a word, he lifted one arm and beckoned the others to join him. One by one the guests slowly walked up the stairs. When they reached the landing, Lord Strathmore started walking towards a large, nail studded door at the far end of the corridor. He opened it with a heavy iron key and one by one they filed through.

As they made their way along another passage, each man was thinking about the sights they were about to see. Would they really find the skeletons of those dead men from so many years ago? What about all the other ghosts that had been seen around the castle? Perhaps *they* would be in the Haunted Room? Or maybe there was something else in there that no-one knew anything about?

They found that their steps were getting heavier and heavier. Also, the ghastly noises seemed to be getting louder and louder. The corridor felt icier by the minute and the night seemed to grow darker than before!

At the end of the corridor, Lord Strathmore opened another door to reveal a narrow winding staircase rising steeply to the next floor.

"It's a long walk, gentlemen," he said, and stood back for his guests to pass through the door.

They were all becoming increasingly scared!

Let us leave Lord Strathmore and his guests for just a moment. As they are making their way, very slowly, from one end of the castle to the other, their minds are filled with terrible visions of the possible horrors locked into Haunted Room. But what they don't know is that behind its door, they may find something other people have already seen—though all of them wished they hadn't!

Glamis Castle is supposed to have its own monster! Sometime around 1800, a baby was born to the Glamis family that was hideously deformed. He had no neck, only minute arms and legs, and looked like a flabby egg. But he was immensely strong, and a special room had to be built for him in the castle where he was hidden away so no-one could see him. Terrible are the tales of his behaviour and the horrific effect he had on anyone who saw him!

At one time, only the Earl of Strathmore, the family lawyer and the factor of the estate knew he existed. But each time a son became twenty-one, he was also let into the secret. The monster lived for a very long time, so the knowledge of his existence was handed down from generation to generation. But what happened to him? That is the question you should keep in the back of your mind as we rejoin the adventurers going to look in the Haunted Room. Perhaps he is still there?

A thunder storm suddenly broke over the castle. Flashes of lightning shot past the windows and rolls of thunder boomed around the battlements. Each of the guests grabbed hold of the nearest person for support. They were *terrified*!

Lord Strathmore had led them along corridor after corridor and up one staircase after another. Each room they passed through was darker and more gloomy than the one before. And each step they took seemed to bring the ghostly sounds closer and louder.

Finally they arrived outside a door which, unlike all the others, Lord Strathmore didn't open straightaway. This was the Haunted Room. They were all wondering what horrible sight would meet their eyes when the door was opened? Would it be skeletons, ghosts, monsters, apparitions or what?

"Are you ready gentlemen?" asked Lord Strathmore.

His guests could only just hear him above the horrific sounds that were roaring from behind the closed door. They, nodded dumbly.

"Then let us see what we shall see." The Lord slowly took from his pocket a large rusty key. Very carefully, because his hands were shaking with fear, he inserted it in the lock. He had turned an ashen grey colour and his hair seemed to be standing on end. His guests tried hard to control their shaking bodies.

Then it happened!

Lord Strathmore turned the key in the lock and with one swift movement flung open the door. It seemed as though the hounds of hell had been released! There was so much noise and confusion, not one of the guests could afterwards say what had really happened! There was shouting, there was screaming, there was yelling and horrific unearthly sounds! Lord Strathmore looked into the Haunted Room then dropped back in a dead faint into the arms of his companions—and the door slammed shut!

Never would the Lord say what he had seen in the room. In fact he wouldn't open his lips on the subject ever afterwards. But one thing he did do instantly, he had the room bricked up so that no-one else would see what he had seen!

DID SHE EXIST?

*Most of the ghosts who pop up in this book, are
ghosts of people who have died, but here's a very
odd story about a woman who appeared to be perfectly normal to her daughter, though nobody else
thought she existed. In other words, she was a ghost
when she was still alive!!! Odd? Read on!*

In 1889, an enormous fair was held in Paris which
was known as the "Great Exhibition". The city was
full of businessmen and tourists, and most of the
hotels were fully booked.

In May of that year, an English woman and her
daughter landed in Marseilles after a journey from
India. They travelled to Paris where they had
booked two single rooms in one of the city's most

famous hotels. When they arrived they both signed the register then were taken up to their rooms.

The mother was given room number 342. It was a very luxurious apartment with a high-backed sofa, beautiful wallpaper covered with roses, heavy curtains of plum-coloured velvet, an oval satinwood table and a magnificent ormulu clock. Unfortunately, they had hardly arrived at the hotel when the mother was taken ill and had to go to bed.

She became so ill that her daughter called in the hotel doctor. He examined the woman, then asked the daughter some questions. The daughter couldn't speak French but she was able to make herself understood. The doctor then called in the hotel manager and took him to one side where they whispered for a long time in a very excited manner. The doctor then explained to the girl that her mother was seriously ill and could only be cured by a particular medicine available only at the doctor's surgery on the other side of Paris. He said that he would stay with the patient while she went to his surgery in his own carriage.

The city was so full of people and carriages that the journey took a very long time. The girl was getting more and more upset as time passed, but finally she arrived at the doctor's surgery. Unfortunately she had to wait for the medicine to be made up, then suffer an even slower journey back to the hotel. It had taken her four hours to get the medicine.

When she reached the hotel, she rushed up to the manager's desk in the foyer and asked how her mother was. The manager looked at her in surprise. "To whom do you refer, Mademoiselle?" he asked.

The girl was equally puzzled so tried her best to

explain what had happened, and why she had taken so long to get the medicine.

The manager looked at her blankly and replied, "But Mademoiselle, I know nothing of your mother. You arrived here alone."

The girl couldn't believe what she heard. "But we registered here less than six hours ago. Look in the book".

The manager opened the book and found the place where the girl had signed her name. But in the space above, where her mother had signed her name, was the name of a complete stranger.

"But we both signed," cried the girl, "and my mother was given room 342. She's there now. Please take me to her at once."

The manager told her that room 342 was occupied by a French family but, when the girl insisted, he agreed to take her up to it. When he unlocked the door the girl was horrified to find that the room had completely changed. It was empty, apart from the personal belongings of the French family, but there were no plum-coloured curtains, no roses on the wallpaper, no high-backed sofa or an ormulu clock! And no mother!

The girl ran down the stairs in great distress. She found the hotel doctor and asked him what had happened to her mother? The doctor said that he'd never met her before and swore that he'd never attended her mother!

The poor girl didn't know what to do? She contacted the British Ambassador, but when he heard from all the people involved in the story that none of them had heard or seen of the mother, he didn't believe what she said. She next tried the police, then the newspapers, but nobody believed her story.

Eventually she returned to England where she spent the rest of her life in a hospital because the incident had unhinged her mind.

So what had really happened?

A possible explanation is that the mother had contracted the plague when she was in India, and when the doctor recognised the symptoms, he and the manager decided to hide the whole affair because of the damage it would cause to the success of the "Great Exhibition". But could room 342 have been re-decorated and changed completely in just four hours? The mother's body was never found, so what happened to it?

That's for you to make up your own mind!!!

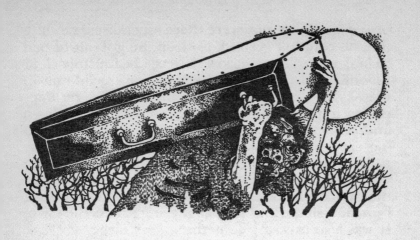

UGLY MAN

Most ghosts appear because they are spirits who can't rest in peace. Either they did something dreadful when they were alive or something dreadful happened to them. But some ghosts appear because they have a purpose or a job to do. Here's one such story.

In 1880, a British diplomat called Lord Dufferin was taking a well-earned rest in Ireland. He was staying in a hotel with a group of friends and thoroughly enjoying his short holiday. He lived a very busy life so was pleased to relax in the heart of the Irish countryside.

One night he woke suddenly from a deep sleep. Normally he slept very well, so he was quite surprised to find himself wide awake. He couldn't hear or see anything, nor were there any noises. Finding that he couldn't go back to sleep, he got out of bed to look out of the window. It was a beautifully clear moonlit night with hundreds of stars twinkling in the sky. As he gazed out of the window, he happened to glance down. Below him was a large lawn and, as he looked, he suddenly saw someone walking across the grass. Lord Dufferin thought it was rather an odd time for anyone to be taking a stroll but, as he continued to watch, he saw something that was even odder. Whoever it was had a strange, hunched shape and was staggering across the lawn. It was also carrying something very large.

Curious to see what was going on, Lord Dufferin put on his dressing gown and went downstairs to go outside. When he reached the lawn, he could see that the figure was a man and he was carrying what looked like a coffin.

"What have you got there!" he shouted.

As the man stopped and turned round to look at him, Lord Dufferin had a great shock! The man's face was dreadfully wizened and distorted. In fact it was the ugliest face he'd ever seen.

Lord Dufferin was about to repeat his question when the man disappeared. Nowhere could he or the coffin be seen. Lord Dufferin was rather alarmed but, not wanting to appear a fool to his friends, he never mentioned the incident and after a few months he forgot that it had ever happened.

Some years later he had to attend a conference in a Paris hotel. After registering at the desk he walked with his private secretary to the lift. The doors were open and the lift attendant was waiting for them. For the second time in his life, Lord Dufferin received a shock! The lift attendant looked straight at him and he saw to his horror that it was the same hideously ugly man he'd seen carrying the coffin in Ireland. He stepped back afraid. His secretary urged him forwards but Lord Dufferin refused to enter the lift. The attendant closed the doors and the lift left the ground floor.

Greatly shaken, Lord Dufferin went to the reception desk to ask who the man was? Nobody knew. In fact nobody working in the hotel knew anything about him.

Just then there was a dreadful shrieking sound— followed by a tremendous crash. The lift had reached the fifth floor of the hotel when, without any reason, the cable had snapped and the lift had fallen and smashed to smithereens on the ground floor. Everybody in the lift was killed, instantly!

Lord Dufferin was never able to discover the identity of the ugly man, all he knew was that this "ghost" had saved his life!!

If you would like to receive a newsletter telling you about our new children's books, fill in the coupon with your name and address and send it to:

Gillian Osband,

Transworld Publishers Ltd,

Century House,

61–63 Uxbridge Road, Ealing,

London, W5 5SA

Name ....

Address ....

....

CHILDREN'S NEWSLETTER

All the books on the previous pages are available at your bookshop or can be ordered direct from Transworld Publishers Ltd., Cash Sales Dept. P.O. Box 11, Falmouth, Cornwall.

Please send full name and address together with cheque or postal order—no currency, and allow 40p per book to cover postage and packing (plus 18p each for additional copies).